Bristol Museum & Art Gallery

Into the Twenty-First Century

Plans for the future include innovative ways of interpreting this rich heritage, foremost of which is the transformation of the Industrial Museum into the Museum of Bristol. This will be accompanied by radical changes to the displays and exhibition spaces in the City Museum & Art Gallery and improved access to reference collections. Thus, with the continuing support and involvement of the local community – including the Friends of Bristol Art Gallery and the Bristol Magpies – the Bristol Museums can look forward with confidence to the future.

The Earth Beneath Our Feet

The City Museum & Art Gallery has a well-deserved reputation for earth history research and its natural sciences collections are among the best and oldest in the country. The emphasis is on specimens from south-west England, especially the Bristol area, but there is also a significant amount of comparative material from other parts of the UK and the rest of the world.

Rocks and Minerals

Minerals, which occur in rocks and deposits throughout the world, come in an astonishing variety of colours and forms – often crystalline and many extremely beautiful. As well as providing the basis of many industries, they also make an important contribution to our understanding of the Earth's crust.

Specimens of all the most common minerals are displayed, together with a fine collection of gemstones. These provide an invaluable reference for the student, although they may also be enjoyed simply for their colour and form. The area around Bristol is itself rich in minerals, some of which formed the basis of local industries, e.g. celestine (strontium sulphate) was commercially extracted for use in the pyrotechnic, sugar-refining and electronic industries.

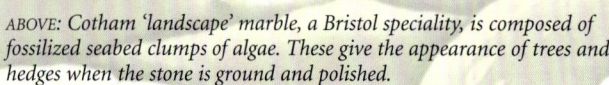

ABOVE: Cotham 'landscape' marble, a Bristol speciality, is composed of fossilized seabed clumps of algae. These give the appearance of trees and hedges when the stone is ground and polished.

LEFT: *The giant Irish deer* (Megaceros giganteus) *became extinct about 10,000 years ago. Its magnificent antlers measured up to 3 metres (10 feet) across.*

BELOW: *The Charmouth ichthyosaur* (Leptopterygius solei), *8 metres (26 feet) long and 200 million years old, was recovered from Lower Jurassic rocks on a cliff on the Dorset coast. A previously unknown species, it is one of the largest of its kind.*

Echoes of the Past

Visitors to the Geology Gallery can trace the history of the Earth from its formation 4,600 million years ago until the present day – a tale illustrated with fossil plants and animals, reconstructions of extinct life-forms and graphic representations of the environmental conditions of these past ages. Examples of most common fossils are displayed, enabling approximate identifications to be made, while an exceptional study collection of 500,000 specimens, 700 of which are type and figured, is available for specialist consultation.

These fossils include Triassic vertebrates from the Bristol area, Jurassic marine vertebrates from Somerset, Wiltshire and Dorset, and Jurassic invertebrates from the south-west generally. There are also even older fossils from the Carboniferous limestone of the Avon Gorge and nearby Mendips, as well as plants, insects and arachnids from the Coal Measures, retrieved from spoil heaps of deserted coal mines.

Sea Dragons

These great reptiles – the plesiosaurs, pliosaurs and ichthyosaurs – were the marine counterparts of the dinosaurs and lived in the Jurassic seas 210–140 million years ago. The remains on display were excavated from deposits in Somerset, Wiltshire and Dorset.

The Living World

The specimens exhibited in the three natural history galleries represent only a fraction of this major regional collection, which includes approximately 650,000 specimens of plants and animals. Many date from the nineteenth century and have historical as well as scientific significance, being records of famous voyages of discovery and of the work of eminent biologists.

Natural History in South-West Britain

This atmospheric gallery comprises a series of 'windows' that open onto aquatic habitats ranging from the open sea to estuarine sand dunes, lakes and rhynes (ditches). Information panels enable the varied plants and animals of these habitats to be readily identified and give details of their life cycles. The decrease in both habitats and species diversity as a result of factors such as changing land use are featured. Displays about the Somerset Levels reveal the secretive wildlife of these internationally important but threatened areas. There is also an interactive map of local wildlife sites and a freshwater aquarium containing fish typical of the south-west region.

World Wildlife

This international collection of birds, mammals, reptiles and insects is mostly grouped geographically. Period dioramas, such as that showing the tiger donated by King George V, bestow a distinct late-Edwardian quality to the gallery. Many specimens date from that era – the age of the explorer and collector – when wildlife was seemingly abundant and conservation was virtually unheard of. Consequently, many are now especially significant because they are representatives of endangered species, or of extinct species, such as the thylacine, or Tasmanian wolf.

British Birds and Mammals

This traditional-style gallery, in which mounted specimens are grouped taxonomically in glass cases, is a useful guide to the species of south-west England. Groupings include birds of prey, warblers and mustelids (stoats and weasels). The accompanying information highlights the ecology, behaviour and conservation status of the animals and, in the case of difficult-to-identify birds, points out the key features.

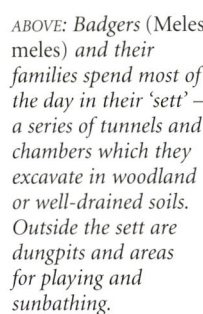

ABOVE: *Badgers* (Meles meles) *and their families spend most of the day in their 'sett' – a series of tunnels and chambers which they excavate in woodland or well-drained soils. Outside the sett are dungpits and areas for playing and sunbathing.*

LEFT: *The fields and rhynes (ditches) of the Somerset Levels provide a rich variety of habitats and are home to many birds, such as barn owls, lapwings and snipe.*

INSET LEFT: *Burchell's zebra* (Equus quagga burchelli) *is one of two subspecies of the plains zebra, which were found in the southern tip of Africa. Both are now extinct.*

Bristol Regional Environmental Records Centre (BRERC)

Housed in the Regency stables of Ashton Court Mansion since 1990, BRERC is responsible for maintaining the database of environmental records for what was formerly the county of Avon. Records cover wildlife and geology and are collected from both individuals and organizations.

From Prehistory to the Present Day

South-west Britain, and Bristol in particular, has a rich history which is reflected by the collections on display in the South-West Archaeology Gallery. These have been steadily growing since 1825 and now amount to several thousand objects. During the nineteenth century, items were mainly derived from individual collections and amateur archaeologists, but since 1899 they have increasingly come from professional excavations.

Prehistory

Artefacts dating from the Palaeolithic period (Stone Age) to the end of the Roman occupation are displayed chronologically to show the development of society over time and include stone axes, arrowheads, prehistoric metalwork, and domestic and funerary pottery. Of special note are the Pool Farm cist (tomb) slab and the Bronze Age urns from the Deverel Barrow in Dorset, one of the two type sites for the Deverel Rimbury 'culture' in southern England.

The Roman Occupation

Although Bristol was not a Roman town, there is evidence of Roman settlement in and around the city, and a small military port was established at Sea Mills (Abonae), which later developed into a larger civilian settlement. The displays explain the impact of Roman occupation in the south-west, with artefacts from a variety of local sites. The finds from villas, such as Brislington, and from religious sites, like that at Nettleton, illustrate all aspects of Roman life, work and death.

ABOVE: *This early 13th-century lead-glazed jug, excavated at Peter Street, Bristol, was made at the Ham Green kilns. The applied decoration shows an archer and his dog in pursuit of a deer.*

Medieval Times

By the Middle Ages, Bristol was second in importance only to London and the displays include a small amount of medieval and later material, particularly ceramic jugs made locally at Redcliffe and Ham Green. Medieval material is also incorporated into a 'timescale' display, illustrating the development of Bristol and its region in relation to world events. Medieval collections showing Bristol as a major centre of trade and industry are mainly in store, but may be viewed by appointment.

RIGHT: *This wall-slab from a stone cist is decorated with carvings of human footprints and cup-marks. It comes from an Early Bronze Age round barrow at Pool Farm, West Harptree, Somerset.*

ABOVE: *The Orpheus pavement from Newton St Loe, which was acquired in 1851, is one of only nine such mosaics known in Britain. This reproduction is taken from a life-sized tracing made by Great Western Railways engineer Thomas Marsh in 1837.*

King's Weston Roman Villa

This third- to fourth-century villa was discovered during construction work in 1947. The site consists principally of the stone foundation walls of what was probably a large Romano-British farmhouse on an agricultural estate. Although much was destroyed, the 13 remaining rooms incorporate a hypocaust-heated room, a small bath suite and mosaic floors. Finds from the excavation are displayed in the South-West Archaeology Gallery.

Ancient Mediterranean Civilizations

The City Museum & Art Gallery holds a large number of antiquities from the Mediterranean area, those from Ancient Egypt and Assyria being especially significant.

Ancient Egypt

Death, ritual and domestic life are all represented in this collection, which ranges from mummies and coffins to children's toys, and from pre-dynastic pots up to 5,000 years old to beautiful woven clothing from the Copts of the fourth century AD. Bristol owes much of this collection to Amelia Edwards (1831–92), Victorian novelist and lover of Egypt. Her concerns about the destructive behaviour of tourists and locals led to the founding of the Egyptian Exploration Society, whose aim was to further the scientific excavation and study of Egyptian ruins. Bristol Museum received a share of the finds from many excavations and still receives occasional donations from the Society.

The Assyrian Empire

The Museum is fortunate in possessing three fine wall decorations from a royal Assyrian palace. They originate from the north-western palace of Ashurnasipal II (884–859 BC) at Nimrud (in present-day Iraq), which was excavated in 1845 by Sir Henry Layard, who shipped many of the wall-panels to the British Museum in London. Sir Henry Rawlinson, who continued the investigation, shipped other panels to England, including three to Bristol, where he was educated. Smaller pieces from Assyria and Babylon include cylinder seals and figurines, as well as ivory carvings, in Egyptian style, which were part of the tribute paid by the Egyptians to the Assyrians, who were then their overlords.

Ancient Greeks and Romans

Fine pottery from Greece (copied in Italy) and fragments of mosaic from Italy are the mainstay of these collections. Some of the items in James Bomford's collection of ancient glass are Roman, while other pieces are from Syria, where glass was first made, Egypt and northern Europe. The delicate jugs, bowls, flasks, beads and drinking glasses demonstrate the skill of these ancient glass-workers.

ABOVE: *Giovanni Belzoni (1778–1823) found the tomb of the Pharaoh Seti I in 1819. He copied the wall decorations, exhibiting a model in London, and his paintings are an important record of the since-damaged tomb.*

LEFT: *This magnificent wall-panel, one of three that lined two rooms in the palace of Ashurnasipal II, features the king and protective gods in shallow relief. The cuneiform text praises the warrior king and his victories.*

RIGHT: *The Amasis painter who made this wine jug, or oinochöe, was one of the great masters of the Athenian black-figure style.*

The Fawcett Collection
Dr Hugh Fawcett specialized in antiquities made of stone and copper alloy. His collection ranges from Palaeolithic hand-axes from northern Europe and Bronze Age jewellery to copper-alloy axes from Luristan, bow brooches from the Roman Empire and mirrors from China.

Around the World

The ethnography collection includes material from the Americas, Africa and the Pacific. Some of the earliest pieces were acquired by armchair anthropologists who never left Bristol but who made the most of having a bustling port on their doorstep, and the Museum subsequently benefited from their interests.

Among the outstanding items donated by nineteenth-century collectors are the eighteenth-century North American Indian beaded pouch and hide clothing, the gift of eye-surgeon Henry Goldwyer, and the Inuit coat, fashioned from sea-otter intestines, given by Benjamin Rotch.

Many other items were donated by people associated with the British colonies: missionaries in the Congo and Nigeria, district officers in Tanzania (then Tanganyika) and naval officers in the Pacific. They did not collect in any scientific manner but bought, bartered and took what attracted them. This has given a haphazard assemblage, which is nonetheless full of interest, beauty and fascination, from the huge bark-cloth masks from New Guinea to a ball of string from the Congo.

This material from the colonial era is balanced by a programme of contemporary collecting aimed at bringing the collections up to date. Among the new acquisitions are knitted hats from Bolivia and Peru, baskets from Zimbabwe, pottery and tinware from Mexico, resist-dyed fabrics from Nigeria, a plastic water-pot from Guatemala, a lemonade bottle of gin from Mozambique, tableware from Tbilisi in Georgia, and a machete from Nicaragua.

Adela Breton (1849–1923) travelled and worked in Mexico where she studied frescoes and sculpture from Mayan ruins. Her copies of wall-paintings at several sites are now the only record of the decorations which have almost vanished within 75 years. This watercolour is of the Pyramid of the Niches at El Tajin, which dates from c.AD 150 to AD 900.

RIGHT: *A 16th-century bronze head of an oba (king) from Benin City, now in Nigeria. The eyes and tribal marks are inlaid with iron.*

10

Money, Medals and Militaria

The coin collection comprises a range of gold and silver coins officially minted in Bristol from Saxon times until 1697, a series of eighteenth- and nineteenth-century tokens, and Roman and other coins found during excavations throughout the city. Most of the medals in the collection were awarded to Bristol men who fought in the French wars of the eighteenth century, the Indian Mutiny and the Crimea. The Museum also holds a miscellany of military items, such as uniforms, drums and colours, mostly related to local volunteer militias or the Glosters regiment. Other items of local interest include civilian awards given for public service, such as civil defence and life-saving.

ABOVE: *Gold noble of Edward IV (1461–70), worth 6s 8d (or 34p). The reverse (tail) shows a medieval ship and in the waves is a 'B' for the Bristol Mint.*

Eastern Art

The collection of Eastern art includes items from the Far East, south and south-east Asia, India and the Islamic world, and is of international importance. Awarded designated status, it is considered to be one of the finest outside London, while the collection of Chinese glass tableware may well be the largest outside China. The City Museum & Art Gallery is indebted to Max Schiller for his 1946 bequest of ceramics, jades and bronzes, paintings, furniture and carpets which he collected with his brother Ferdinand. Since then the collections have been greatly expanded.

Chinese Glass

Small glass objects, such as beads, were made in China from the fifth century BC and the craft developed dramatically during the Manchu Qing dynasty (1644–1912). Beautiful, often large, decorated glasses have continued to be blown or cut until the present day. The collection includes wonderful examples of many of the decorative techniques and colours as well as the high artistry of the glass-makers of China. Some 290 pieces, dating from the second to third centuries AD until this century, were donated by Mr H.R. Burrows Abbey in 1950, through the National Art Collection Fund.

Chinese Ceramics

The range of Chinese ceramics is also exceptional, ranging from Neolithic vessels dated c.2500 BC to twentieth-century items, and leaves us in awe of the mastery of form and glaze, and controlled firing, which only a few potters have ever attained. The Schiller collection has unique examples of the wares of the Tang (AD 618–907) and Song (AD 960–1280) dynasties, the period of its greatest strength. The Chinese porcelain of two or three centuries ago was so highly prized by European patrons that, in the eighteenth century, a flourishing repair industry arose in Bristol and elsewhere, of which this Museum has gathered an interesting study collection.

Japanese Prints

The City Museum & Art Gallery holds about 600 Japanese prints, including works by Harunobu (c.1725–70), Hokusai (1760–1849) – including two versions of his famous tidal wave – and Hiroshige (1797–1858). Acquired in the 1950s and 1960s, the collection has an exceptionally high proportion of eighteenth-century artists.

ABOVE: One of a pair of shallow dishes from the K'ang Hsi period. It is decorated with underglaze blue and features a pair of surprised lovers.

LEFT: This cylindrical vessel, possibly a brush pot, features a green overlay on translucent bubbly glass and is mounted on a ground-out foot-ring. It was made in China, probably during the 19th century.

RIGHT: Japanese wood-block print of actor Segawa Kikunojo III in female role, by Katsukawa Sunshō (1762–92).

Fine Art

The Art Gallery provides a broad overview of both British and continental European painting and, thanks to the Schiller bequest of 1946, houses a number of significant Old Masters. More unexpected is the gallery devoted entirely to the French School. Of the total collection of some 18,000 paintings, drawings, watercolours, prints and sculptures, only about 200 are displayed in the Art Gallery, where the glass roof enables them to be viewed under ideal conditions of natural light. A further selection is exhibited at the Georgian House, the Red Lodge and Blaise Castle House Museum.

French School

The Two Sisters, c.1889, a pastel by the French Impressionist Pierre Augustus Renoir.

The collection of French paintings is acknowledged as one of the finest in a provincial gallery and includes works by the Le Nain Brothers (mid-seventeenth century), Delacroix (1798–1863), Courbet (1819–77), Redon (1840–1916), Seurat (1859–91) and Vuillard (1868–1940). Outstanding among the several French masterpieces is *The Donkey Ride* – Eva Gonzales' portrait of her languid-eyed sister and the only work by this woman Impressionist in any British public collection. There is also a signed landscape by the obscure classical artist Etienne Rendu, dated 1652, and a portrait of Madame Bruguière by the French historical painter Baron Gros (1771–1835). Landscapes, sea views and interiors bring a flavour of France and the French vividly to Bristol, as do the works of Impressionists, such as Renoir (1814–1919) and Sisley (1839–99).

Old Masters

This gallery is particularly strong in the Italian School, with works by the Florentine artist Taddeo Gaddi (c.1300–66) and Giovanni Bellini (c.1430–1516), the greatest Venetian artist of his time. There are two detailed studies of the lagoon at Venice by Bernardo Bellotto (1720–80), nephew of Canaletto, one of which is a *capriccio*, or imaginary scene. The Dutch School is well represented and the end of the gallery is dominated by the large *Noah's Ark* by Jan Griffier, (c.1645–1718). There are also some Flemish and German paintings, such as *The Nativity* by Jacob Jordaens (1593–1678) and a striking portrait of *Martin Luther* by Lucas Cranach (1472–1553).

RIGHT: *The immense* Noah's Ark, c.1710, by Jan Griffier, one of the many Dutch artists who were working in England in the late 17th century. It hung in the Great Hall at Nettlecombe Court in Somerset for 300 years.

Fine Art

British Collection

This impressive collection, which includes the Bristol School, is housed in four galleries and spans four centuries. Among the earliest works are some interesting Jacobean portraits by Larkin (1580–1619) and Peake (c.1551–1619), while portraits by Gainsborough (1727–88), Reynolds (1723–92) and Lawrence (1769–1830) contrast with such rustic portrayals as *The Swineherd* by James Ward (1769–1859).

The modest but important Victorian collection includes works by major artists, such as Burne-Jones (1833–98), Millais (1829–96), Tissot (1836–1902) – a French painter noted for his portrayals of Victorian life – and others, such as Bristol's W.J. Müller (1812–45).

Twentieth-century British painting is particularly well represented and features works by leading British artists, such as Sickert (1860–1942), Gilman (1878–1919), Nicholson (1894–1982), Lanyon (1918–64) and Inshaw (b.1943). The depictions, by Piper (1903–92), of Bristol churches bombed during World War II are of especial interest locally. A small selection of 1960s' abstracts is also displayed.

Eve at the Fountain by Edward Hodges Baily (1788–1867). This Bristol-born sculptor produced the statue of Nelson in Trafalgar Square as well as many other well-known London statues.

Bristol School

The dramatic cliffs and secluded valleys of the Avon Gorge inspired an accomplished school of local painters, the most well known being Francis Danby (1793–1861), and many of their often unashamedly romantic works are displayed in the Art Gallery. Through their eyes, it is also possible to rediscover medieval and Georgian Bristol – some of which remains largely unaltered – while portraits by local artists such as Rolinda Sharples and Nathan Cooper Branwhite recall some of the city's personalities.

In the 1820s, Bristol merchant and collector George Weare Braikenridge (1775–1856) had the vision to commission a group of talented Bristol watercolourists to record the city before modernization took its toll. The 1,500 drawings which resulted, together with some 3,500 others, provide a unique portrayal of the city's past as well as a vital reference for students of local history.

View on the Avon at Hotwells, c.1831, by Samuel Jackson, features Brunel's original design for the Clifton Suspension Bridge, which was not completed until 1864.

Sculpture

In addition to some early works, such as the terracotta study of Edward Colston by Michael Rysbrack (1694–1770) and the brilliant pieces by Gaudier-Brzescka (1891–1915), there is a small selection of the work of twentieth-century British sculptors, including Elisabeth Frink (1930–93), Richard Long (b.1945) and David Nash (b.1945).

Themes of chivalry were popular among Victorian artists and La Belle Dame Sans Merci, the work of Sir Frank Dicksee (1853–1928), shows an innovative use of vibrant colour and dramatic spatial construction.

The Decorative Arts

Bristol holds an important place in the history of pottery and glass manufacture, and these wares are well represented in the displays, together with some fine examples of domestic and ecclesiastical silverware. A selection of textiles, lacquered snuffboxes, carved ivories and furniture is held in the Museum's reserve collections.

Ceramics

As Bristol produced most types of ceramic over a long period, the collection is fairly comprehensive and that of English delftware is the largest in the country. This heavy but decorative tin-glazed earthenware was made in Bristol and at Brislington, then a rural parish in north Somerset, from c.1640 to c.1785. As changing fashion demanded lighter, cream-coloured and painted tableware, Bristol responded, supplying it in every shape and size. Soft-paste porcelain was produced from 1748 to 1751 by Benjamin Lund and there is a fine loan collection of Lund's Bristol/early Worcester wares. The first English hard-paste, or true, porcelain was made in Bristol in the 1760s and a factory was in production from 1770 until 1778. The works of William Cookworthy and Richard Champion are outstanding and the best wares exhibit some of the finest gilding of this era.

Thereafter, individual quality gave way to mass production, such as bricks and drainpipes. Pountney's continued to produce tableware into the 1960s, while the firms of Price and Powell, who eventually amalgamated, produced stoneware until November 1940. Today, the City Museum & Art Gallery continues to develop these local collections, as well as introducing work by many leading studio potters.

LEFT: *The 'Raby' vase, of porcelain with enamelled and gilded decoration, was made at the Bristol Pottery, c.1840. It is one of Edward Raby's largest and most ambitious works, and one of the Bristol Pottery's masterpieces.*

RIGHT: *A delft dish made in Bristol, c. 1730.*

ABOVE: *This set of four pearlware tiles, decorated with enamel, is signed 'Feby 15 1820 W. Fifield' and was made at the Bristol Pottery. It shows the Pottery from the east, with two biscuit kilns (left) and two glazing kilns (right). The tower of Temple Church can be seen in the background.*

ABOVE: *The St Werburgh's Church plate is one of the earliest sets of communion plate in England, and the finest from all the Bristol churches. The ewer (left), flagon (right) and tazza (centre) shown here are all of silver-gilt and were donated to the church in the 1620s.*

Silverware

Exhibits include a representative selection of seventeenth-, eighteenth- and nineteenth-century silverware. Teapots and coffeepots, cruets and flatware, jugs and candlesticks, all designed to enhance the tables of the wealthy, embody some of the best work that British silversmiths were able to achieve, while the rare Bristol-made and hallmarked silver should not be missed.

The Decorative Arts

Glass

Bristol glass is world-famous and features prominently in the displays, but much is unmarked and so impossible to identify with any certainty. Apart from a few fragments excavated locally, pre-eighteenth-century glass is poorly represented, although the Lazarus collection demonstrates the impressive range of drinking glasses which was made in Britain between 1685 and 1800.

The inspiration for the famous 'Bristol Blue' glass came in the second half of the eighteenth century, when supplies of smalt, a pigment of cobalt, were first imported into Bristol. Examples of this glassware on display include signed vessels by Isaac Jacobs (1757–1835). The nineteenth century saw the introduction of colourless cut glass, while window and bottle-glass were produced in Bristol and also at the nearby Nailsea glassworks.

In addition to locally manufactured glass, the City Museum & Art Gallery also boasts a superb array of mid-nineteenth-century French glass paperweights, as well as items by such eminent glass-workers as Gallé (1846–1904) and Herman (b.1936).

Jewellery

The Georgian and Victorian jewellery on display tell of both technical achievement and patronage. As pieces by Wendy Ramshaw and her contemporaries show, modern jewellery is as much a craft as an art, and precious stones and metals are often supplemented with synthetic materials.

ABOVE: These three fine decanters of 'Bristol Blue' glass are signed 'I. Jacobs, Bristol' and were made c.1805.

BELOW: The gold-and-pearl bangle with dog-collar plaque by René Lalique (1860–1945) is one of the finest works in the Bristol collection.

ABOVE: Mid-18th century drinking glasses from the Peter Lazarus collection.

Furniture

There is a representative collection of seventeenth- to nineteenth-century furniture, much of which is displayed in the period settings of the Red Lodge and the Georgian House. Of particular note are a walnut bureau of *c.*1730, with a host of secret drawers, at the Red Lodge and an unusual double-secretaire bookcase at the Georgian House. A small collection of later nineteenth- and twentieth-century furniture, which is currently not on display, includes important examples by the influential Bristol-born architect and designer, E.W. Godwin.

BELOW: *This spectacular double-secretaire bookcase, dating from c.1800, can be seen in the library of the Georgian House.*

The Industrial Museum

Housed in a typical post-war dockside warehouse, the Industrial Museum is a bustling place, with collections demonstrating the wide variety of Bristol's trades and industries. On the dockside are a selection of cranes and a railway operated by two steam locomotives, *Portbury* and *Henbury*, while in the dock itself are two tugs and a fire-boat, all Bristol-built.

Road and Rail

This gallery houses examples of the many vehicles produced in Bristol since the mid-nineteenth century. The earliest horse-drawn vehicles range from the Lord Mayor's state coach to the first holiday caravan, while the Grenville steam carriage, built *c.*1880, is one of the oldest working steam-powered vehicles. With the advent of the internal combustion engine, Bristol began to produce buses, bus chassis, lorries, cars and motorcycles, such as the Lodekka omnibus and Douglas motorcycles. Also on display is a section of broad-gauge railway carriage and a working gauge-one model railway.

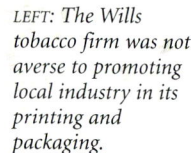

LEFT: *The Wills tobacco firm was not averse to promoting local industry in its printing and packaging.*

Printing and Packaging

Many local companies, especially tobacco and confectionery producers, were reliant on the printing and packaging industries and the gallery houses a variety of working machinery, some Bristol-made. There is also a reconstruction of a printer's workshop, while the stone frieze around the gallery walls, taken from the Robinson factory, depicts its printing and packaging operations.

The Power to Fly

Bristol's long-established aerospace industry is represented by a definitive collection of aero-engines, a genuine *Sycamore* helicopter and a mock-up of a *Concorde* cockpit. There are also 1:72 scale models of most of the aircraft produced in Bristol, from the tiny *Babe* to the enormous *Brabazon*, and paintings of the *Brabazon* project by Terence Cuneo.

ABOVE: *The 1937 steam locomotive* Henbury *was built by Bristol manufacturers Thos. Peckett & Sons Ltd and now regularly gives passengers rides along the dockside.*

LEFT: *The Port of Bristol Gallery features many stunning model ships, all made with great attention to detail.*

RIGHT: *Scipio Africanus, servant to the Earl of Suffolk and Bindon, died in 1720 when 18 years old and is buried in Henbury churchyard outside Bristol.*

The Port of Bristol

Model ships and reconstructions trace the 300-year history of the port from Cabot's departure in 1497 to seek a passage to the Orient, through the years of trade with Africa and the East Indies in the eighteenth century, to the building of Royal Portbury dock in the 1970s and thence to the present day.

Trans-Atlantic Slavery

Confronting myths and confounding misconceptions, this exhibition gives life and faces to those caught up in the triangular trade between Britain, Africa and the Caribbean, and concludes with the legacy of the slave trade and its implications for people today.

BELOW: *This plan of the Liverpool slave ship* Brookes *shows how tightly slaves were packed in the hold.*

The Georgian House

Bristol's colourful and prosperous history is reflected in the lifestyles of its former inhabitants, many of whom were involved in trade and industry. The Georgian House is one of two period-house museums that provide a fascinating insight into the everyday existence of both masters and servants alike.

This typical middle-class merchant's dwelling was built c.1790 for John Pinney, who was a sugar-grower and West India merchant. Presented to the city in 1937, it was opened as a period-house museum in 1939. Its appearance from the street is deceptive: it actually consists of six storeys!

Research into the Pinney family papers has enabled the rooms to be restored to their original functions and redecorated and furnished in the style of the period. These rooms range from the basement kitchen, complete with pots and pans and a roasting spit, to the elegant drawing rooms and the bedroom with its fine views of the city and the docks.

ABOVE: *The fireplace is the heart of the Georgian House kitchen. China was still very expensive so the cooking pots and utensils were made of metal or wood.*

BELOW: *The drawing room of the Georgian House is decorated according to the original 1790s' colour scheme and the furniture is arranged around the walls with typical Georgian formality.*

The Great Oak Room on the first floor of the Red Lodge, with its magnificent panelling, is one of the finest Elizabethan rooms in the south-west.

The Red Lodge

This Elizabethan lodge was built c.1590 and despite substantial alterations around 1730, especially to the exterior, three of the original oak-panelled rooms survive relatively intact. Most notable is the Great Oak Room – considered to be one of the finest rooms of this period in the south-west. Another room is devoted to Mary Carpenter who, in 1854, here set up the country's first reform school for girls, while an impressive collection of seventeenth-century French portrait engravings is housed in the Print Room.

The furniture, which is representative of the seventeenth and early eighteenth centuries, includes a bed dating from 1600 and a magnificent bureau-cabinet dating from c.1730. What remained of the original gardens was laid out in the style of a Tudor knot-garden in 1983, and all the plants used were known in England by the seventeenth century.

LEFT: *The Red Lodge was completed in about 1590 and was home to a succession of local families, as well as a girls' reformatory, before becoming a branch museum in 1920. The Tudor-style knot-garden was laid out in 1983.*

Blaise Castle House Museum

Blaise 'Castle' was built as a folly in 1766 by Thomas Farr, owner of the Blaise Estate, and was made famous by Jane Austen, who featured it in *Northanger Abbey*.

Blaise Castle House was built in 1796–98 for John Harford, a wealthy Bristol merchant and banker, who was also responsible for the addition of Blaise hamlet, the dairy and the conservatory, which were all designed by Regency architect John Nash. The picture gallery, designed by Charles Cockerell and now restored to its mid-Victorian glory, was added in 1832/33.

Displays include a history of Blaise, featuring Humphry Repton's 1796 'Red Book' of plans for the Estate, and 'Bristol at Home', an exhibition of domestic equipment and furnishings, toys, costume, and other items of everyday life in the Bristol area between about 1800 and 1950.

ABOVE: *The exhibition of domestic equipment at Blaise Castle House Museum includes an interesting collection of sanitary ware.*

LEFT: *The miniature has a universal appeal and the detail shown in this dolls' house will fascinate adults and children alike.*

Museum Services

Behind the Scenes

The Bristol Museums hold about 4 million items in all and the extensive reserves include nationally important reference collections, as well as literature, archive and photographic material. These can be made available for study purposes on request. Curators are also available, by appointment, to give advice on specific items.

ABOVE: *The variety of regular children's activities held by the Museum are enthusiastically attended.*

Services for Schools and the Community

At all Museum sites the Curriculum Support team runs schools' workshops, handling and role-playing sessions, and IN-SETS (In-Service Training) for teachers. It also encourages independent visits on the many aspects of the Museums' collections that are relevant to the National Curriculum.

The Outreach team works on a variety of projects, both within the Museums and in the community. These include producing one-off displays and community displays complementing larger exhibitions, organizing regular children's holiday and family activities and workshops.

Museum Services

Special Exhibitions and Events

A changing programme of special exhibitions provides regular opportunities to rotate outstanding objects in the permanent collections, as well as introducing exhibitions on less conventional subjects and annual local favourites. There is also the new role of exhibiting work from the Museums' community projects.

Regular free events include:
- the annual series of Winter Lectures, at which acknowledged authorities speak on a variety of subjects relevant to the exhibitions, collections and work of the Museums and Art Gallery
- the Summer Walks, led by local history and wildlife experts
- family activity days on the first Sunday of each month
- holiday activities at the branch museums.

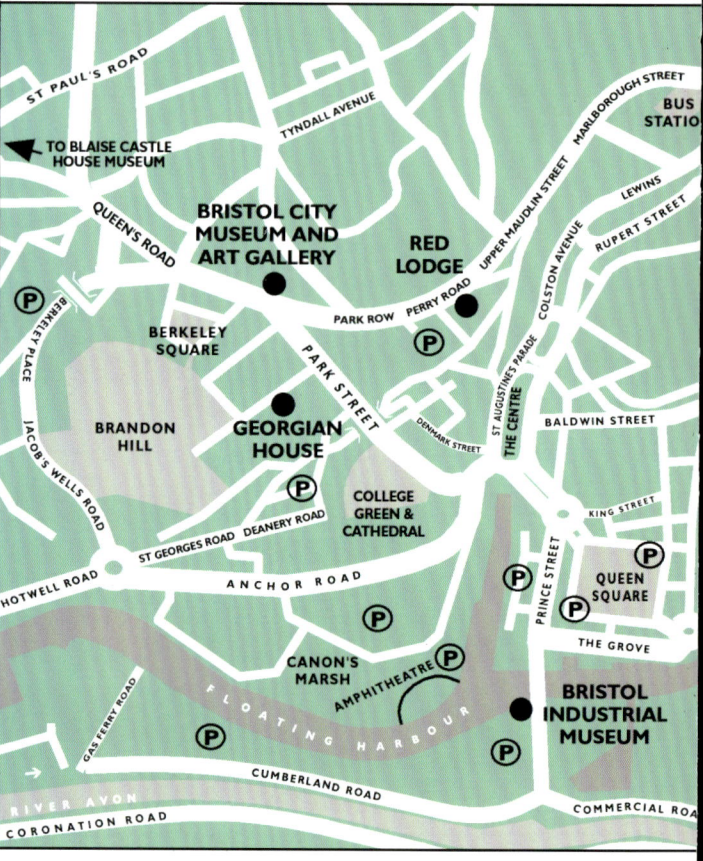

LEFT: *Visitors to the re-enactments at the Georgian House can learn about life for slaves and slave-owners and their families in the 1790s.*

Visitor Facilities

The City Museum & Art Gallery café offers a selection of light refreshments and the shop stocks a range of quality gifts and souvenirs; there are smaller shops at Blaise Castle House and the Industrial Museums.

Museums Supporters' Groups

Established in 1948, the Friends of Bristol Art Gallery is one of two groups supporting Bristol Museum Services, the other being the Bristol Magpies. The Friends arrange lectures, events, educational activities and a social programme for members, as well as actively supporting the work of the City Museum & Art Gallery, especially in the areas of fine, decorative and Eastern arts. New members are always welcome.